LIFE IS SHORT
And So Is This Book

Brief thoughts on making the most of your life

Peter Atkins

To Sam and Lillie - who have made my short life wonderful.

INTRODUCTION

Life is short. You can, if you work hard and are lucky, get more of almost anything, but you can't get more time. Time only goes one way. The average American has a lifespan of less than 30,000 days. So how you choose to live matters.

That's the topic of this book. I don't pretend to have all the answers. I'm still learning every day, and many of the good ideas here I've picked up from other people either directly or by reading. But this is what's worked for me.

Like life, this book is short. Many books I read could communicate their ideas in fewer pages. So I've tried to be brief in line with the wise person who noted: *"If I'd had more time I would have written a shorter letter".*

I don't think brevity implies lack of content. The concepts here have improved the quality of my life, and I hope they're useful to you as well.

Using these concepts, I have created a life I love. My job doesn't feel like work. I love and respect the people with whom I spend time. And I'm also passionate about my life outside work. I've learned how to create a balance that makes me happy between work and other interests, including my family, friends and exercise. Sadly I think that's rare. And yet, while I know I'm lucky, most people can work towards those goals in their own lives.

My interest in making the most of my life began when I was just starting college, but when I was in my mid-thirties a boss I admired died of cancer. He was young. He had a great wife; he had three young children; he had a fantastic career -- he had everything in life. He just didn't have enough time. So, while I'd often thought about how to get the most out of life, the death of someone so young and vital increased my sense of urgency to act on it.

One of the things I've always wanted to do was to work for myself. As a result, I left an exciting job at Microsoft in 2001 amidst the Internet bust to found the investing firm I now run. It was hard to do, both financially and emotionally. When I left Microsoft, many people – friends, family, and even some of the press - thought I was deluding myself to start a fund focused on Internet-related companies during a market crash. A press quote from the time said: *Call him a little crazy. Call him a little nuts.* I'd never seen that type of coverage before. And, in a sense, the press was right; the business wasn't easy to start. Fortunately, from a vantage point of ten years down the road, it's worked out quite well.

A key part of my job is reading and thinking about a broad variety of topics. So writing this book was relatively easy. It's even easier to read. But, like many things in life, actually executing each day on these concepts is extremely difficult. With thanks to Thomas Edison, life is 1% inspiration and 99% perspiration. Even so, I hope you have fun perspiring.

Peter Atkins
Seattle, WA

December, 2010

CONTENTS

1

CREATE SPACE

Life moves pretty fast.
If you don't stop to look around once in a while you could miss it.

- From the movie, Ferris Bueller's Day Off

We all approach life in different ways. Some ways allow more time to think, to be creative, to do what's important, and to spend time with friends. I'll give you an example.

A friend of mine used to be the CEO of a well-known Internet company. He once told me he found it funny that the busiest people on his team were always the people to whom he could give more work, while the ones who accomplished less had little time for anything (often including their existing responsibilities).

I've found this is an important observation. It's often the most successful people I know who are most efficient with their time and who always seem to have time to think and to do more. The trick is people who are most productive tend to say no to things that are unimportant to them and focus on what they believe matters. When you think about it, how could it be any other way?

Of course, activity by itself doesn't equal accomplishment, and certainly not success -- being busy just means being busy. I know many people who work super hard to fill up the spaces in their lives, so they won't have to think. A wise colleague calls this "numbing out". They may accomplish their goals, but they're unlikely to be fulfilled or do truly creative work. I know other people who fill their free time with meaningless activities. They're also busy, but they neither achieve much, nor are they satisfied.

In contrast, I once had a smart boss who told me if I wanted to do my best work, I needed to do fewer things, and really focus on what mattered. That was great advice. Many people confuse *want to* with *have to*. In other words, just because someone else wants you to do something doesn't mean you have to do it. You can't get more time, so how you spend the time you have is critical. Focusing on what matters means saying no to things that don't matter. Otherwise, your life becomes cluttered with distractions.

Technology presents both potential distractions and also great opportunities to use your time better. Technology is a tool. Used properly, it can help you but, like any other tool, it can be mismanaged. If, for example, you spend most of your day responding to email, or text messages, or checking out your friends on social networks, you won't get much done.

A better approach is to decide what you want to do and what is most important. Make lists. Then use technology to assist you, versus allowing it to control you. To execute on this concept requires discipline and practice, but anyone can get better at it, and make real progress if they want to.

One way I like to use technology to save time is, where appropriate, to eliminate meetings and use email instead. I should emphasize 'where appropriate'. Email does a terrible job of conveying subtle emotional content, so meetings are more appropriate for team building, for negotiating, for personal conversations, and for any other situation where it's important to look someone in the eye. But, for some things, email is better.

Mobile devices provide a fantastic way to stay connected and on top of work, wherever you may be. If you have any down time, you can read books or articles, check email, or browse the web from virtually anywhere.

Distractions have increased for reasons beyond new technologies. According to the Bureau of Labor Statistics, about 60% of U.S. families are two-income households, compared with only about one-third in the mid 60's (the statistics are directionally similar in much of the Western world). We're busier and, consequently, are tempted to do lots of things at once.

A number of people I know claim to be great multi-taskers. The brain, however, doesn't work that way; instead it focuses on one activity at a time. If you switch back and forth between multiple tasks, your brain works more slowly than it would if you focused on each activity for a period of time. Albert Einstein said: *It's not that I'm so smart, it's just that I stay with problems longer.* Most of us do the opposite -- with predictable results.

To allow yourself time to think, there are many non-technological tricks to managing information. All of them require you to make choices to focus your energy. I like to set aside blocks of time for specific activities - even to read or chat.

That being said, there are combinations of activities which work together and can make you more productive. For example, I frequently ride an indoor bicycle while reading, since the indoor bicycle takes no mental attention, and it allows me to get exercise at the same time. (Don't try to do the same thing, though, on an outdoor bike!)

Another way to free up time, if you have the option, is to live close to work. For many people, the amount of time spent commuting is huge, and it tends to be quite stressful and, frequently, not super productive. There are usually good reasons people want to live far from work; it's often significantly cheaper, and the schools may be better.

But, if you think about the value of your time, it might not make sense. You might be able to afford a smaller home closer to your job rather than a bigger one with a long commute. And, if you do that, you might have significantly less stress on a daily basis. In fact, when I lived in Manhattan, frequently the most relaxing part of my day was walking to and from my office. It didn't seem like a sacrifice to have a tiny apartment on the third floor of a building without an elevator.

The ultimate reduction in commuting time is working from home – something that is becoming increasingly possible for many people, given the evolution of technology, and the desire of companies to get the most out of their employees while limiting real estate costs. If you have a job which accommodates it, are self-motivated, and have the space and quiet required to work well from home, it can make life considerably more pleasant, and can create more discretionary time. A handful of my colleagues work from home. They all love it -- none would choose to work in an office again.

Making space in your life by using time efficiently also helps nurture creativity. I find it interesting that people who tend to be the most creative have three things in common:

> They're incredibly well prepared in their fields -- they become masters of their domains by practicing for many years, day after day.

> They spend time deeply focused on solving a key problem or key set of problems, no matter the obstacles.

> They allow themselves to step away from the problem(s) on which they're focused, so that insights can come to them in activities such as walking, or looking out on a beautiful scene.

To get great insights absolutely requires hard work, but it also requires space. This is the case because the human mind is not a linear machine. If you don't put in the required effort, you won't be capable of generating good ideas; you won't understand the subject matter. But if you don't give yourself space from the problems on which you are working, you likely will be so worn down you won't generate creative insights. You need both.

In taking walks these days, I try to notice the beauty around me; it helps me think and relax. In fact, I regularly take pictures with my cell phone camera (some are included here) as a reminder to stop and look. It's a simple thing (and my pictures won't win any prizes) but it works.

So to make the most of your life, say no to things that don't matter, work hard at what you love, and occasionally take time away from your core focus to rest so that your mind can be quiet for great insights to come.

Looking out to the Olympic Mountains, Washington

2

TRY NOT TO WORRY

If you can't sleep, then get up and do something instead of lying there worrying.
It's the worry that gets you, not the lack of sleep.

-Dale Carnegie

Worrying, I've found, wastes energy and wastes time; it limits what you can accomplish. I try not to obsess on the past, but to learn from it. I try not to worry about the future, but to prepare for it. And while it's difficult sometimes, I try to take pleasure in the moment, even when bad things happen.

An inspirational woman I know has cancer, yet she finds the beauty in every day and every moment. I don't know many people who are more positive, or go through life with as much curiosity or energy as she does. The last time I saw her was at a dinner party -- she was more engaged than anyone else that evening, constantly asking questions about new technology, and how I thought it would change the world. I also have several friends with Multiple Sclerosis, and they live more restricted (and more painful) lives than most of us, but each seems excited every time we meet. They're clearly trying to get the most out of their limited time left on earth.

The lesson to me is that you can focus on something going well, or something beautiful, or something interesting -- even amidst terrible times.

I try to put things into two buckets: one I can do something about and one I can't. The things I can't do anything about, I try to ignore. There's no use, for example, being jealous of other people's success or good luck; it won't make me any happier. Nor is there any upside in worrying about a bad situation in which I find myself. There is, however, a lot to be gained from considering how I can move to a better place.

I've also noticed it helps to accept the world as it is -- not in the sense that you can't change things (although that is sometimes the case), but in the sense that you need to see reality clearly before you can take effective action. As a professor of mine once said: if you think the table you are sitting at will fly, you have a problem.

Accept that luck and bad luck aren't evenly or fairly distributed, and you can't do anything about that. I have many talented friends in the technology industry who've been paid over the years primarily in stock options. Some have made a great deal of money this way, and frequently they were just lucky to have joined a given company at a certain time. They weren't necessarily more talented than others. They didn't work harder, or contribute more than people who started later than they did. They frequently didn't even have a strong conviction in advance that they'd make a lot of money (although they knew there was a chance they might). They were, relative to their peers, lucky.

There are some things in life you can't change (such as your parents, your height, or the personalities of other adults). For the problems you can impact and you want to alter, think about what you want to accomplish, and try to do that in a pragmatic way. You don't have to change everything overnight. In fact, thinking you can, or should, is likely to lead to failure, or to feeling overwhelmed -- and as a result perhaps doing nothing.

My experience the last ten years illustrates this point. If I'd tried to build my investing business to scale in a short time frame, or worried when stock prices declined, I would have failed. I started investing immediately before September 11th. While prices of Internet stocks then were low relative to their business value, prices dropped significantly for another year and a half during the Internet bust before recovering to sensible levels. I had no idea that would happen. It didn't feel pleasant. My family lost faith in me, and most of my friends thought I was a bit nuts to even invest in the sector. It was only because I stayed focused on understanding the businesses in which I'd invested, and was willing to stick with my convictions over a matter of years, that my ideas worked out well. Over time, other people gained faith in my investing abilities, but it didn't happen overnight. It wasn't easy. And nothing I might have done early on would have changed that.

Lastly, when you make mistakes along the way, as I have at many points in my life, accept them as well. I've tried to learn from my mistakes. They're experience – and they're the sort of experience you won't soon forget.

As Winston Churchill said: *Success is not final, failure is not fatal: it is the courage to continue that counts.*

Sunset from the air; somewhere over western Canada.

3

DON'T DO REALLY DUMB THINGS

All I want to know is where I'm going to die so I'll never go there.

- Charlie Munger

You can't follow Charlie Munger's advice literally. But, as a wise colleague of mine says, sometimes the most important thing to do is to not do anything *really* dumb. I've found this type of inactivity is undervalued in our culture.

Many investors overlook avoiding dumb mistakes. Warren Buffett suggests people approach investing the same way Ted Williams looked at batting: only swing at the pitches in the center of your strike zone. Since there are no called strikes in investing, you should let the others go by. This sounds easy to do, and you'd think most investors would behave this way, but they don't. When many people buy stocks, they tend to think more about the potential upside than what they might lose if things don't go well. By pivoting that thinking and avoiding really dumb ideas -- in investing, in business, and in life – you'll approach problems from a wholly different perspective.

I've used this same mental model to try to avoid too much debt, drinking too much, staying away from people who are bad influences, eating poorly, and not exercising.

I should probably make the distinction here between *really* dumb things, and routine mistakes made in the course of your life. The latter, as I've noted, are certainly painful, but inescapable and useful learning. What do I mean, then, by *really* dumb things? There are two classes: unrecoverable errors and denial.

Unrecoverable errors can screw up your future - like committing a crime and going to prison, or limiting your options by not trying to get the best education available, or making decisions which likely will lead to major health problems or financial destruction. As an extreme example, I know someone who, as a child, accidentally shot his sibling. The sibling never fully recovered and the accidental-shooter never overcame his guilt. As a result, his life has been ruined.

There are many things that are not nearly as dramatic, but can have a similarly negative long-term impact. What you choose to do each day matters. Habits form when we're young, and solidify before we know it. So forming the right habits early is critical, whether that means eating well, exercising, saving money or being honest. As a wise investor I know likes to say, people become "more so" over time.

The second class of dumb thing – denial – is common. Most of us ignore reality in some facet of our lives. It's often easier to believe things will somehow solve themselves, whether we want a lousy job to work out, or we're so desperate to hire someone for a much-needed role we sacrifice on quality, or we overlook obvious issues in someone we're dating (and assume they'll get better over time…or we can help fix them).

These are all examples of wishful thinking. If you notice serious problems in the early stages of a job, or in the hiring process, they're only likely to become magnified as you get to know the situation, or your new colleague better. Ditto in dating. Small problems early on generally don't just resolve themselves with time. And it's impossible to change other adults' personalities, no matter what you may wish.

A well known joke illustrates the point: The biggest mistake men make when they think about getting married is they assume women won't change; the biggest mistake women make is they assume they can change men.

The same warning about wishful thinking is true with exercise and pain. If you start feeling pain while exercising, it's the body's way of telling you to stop. If you battle through it, as many of us do, frequently you'll make the injury worse.

So how can you avoid really dumb things? I try to rely on my gut instincts. Whenever I feel that something might have a really bad outcome, I pay attention to that feeling. Feelings aren't always correct (we fear many things we have little reason to be concerned about in the modern world), but feelings can flag problems that may be difficult to articulate.

Proceeding when there are obvious issues is a dumb thing to do. Even if it's inconvenient or painful, I've learned, I'm better off doing nothing when the only available choice has glaring issues.

Snowshoeing in Whistler, BC.

4

BUILD CHARACTER AND MAKE FRIENDS

Character is like a tree, and reputation like its shadow. The shadow is what we think of it; the tree is the real thing.

- Abraham Lincoln

Character, I've found, is one of the most important things in life. Reputations can be manipulated in the short term, but people tend to get the reputations they deserve over time. Reputations are your personal brand. They're influential in how well you do in both your professional and personal lives.

There are four basic principles that have worked well for me:

Do what you think is right.

Don't follow other people blindly.

Be honest and keep your word.

Admit your mistakes.

If you live your life authentically, keep your word, admit mistakes, and admit what you don't know, you'll find people will trust you more over time, and you'll become wiser too.

When I entered college, I thought most people would adopt similar principles, but I've found that a lot of people succumb to peer pressure and other external forces.

I've met lots of smart people who work very hard. I've met substantially fewer who are also authentic and have integrity. I try to spend my time with the second group. And, generally, I've found that those people are happy and have more real friends.

* * * * *

Inevitably, we take on some of the habits of people with whom we're closest. The people with whom we associate can have a huge impact on the development of our personalities, particularly when we're young. In that light, if you have children, try to be sure their peer groups are healthy ones. Their peers likely will have more influence on the development of your kids' personalities than you will. If that sounds absurd, look at how immigrants' kids develop in a non-immigrant community; they nearly always seem to speak, act and have the values of their peers, and not their immigrant parents. My son, for instance, has a friend whose parents recently emigrated from Japan and moved to Canada. My son's friend doesn't like Japanese food; his favorite things to eat include steak and hamburgers; and he acts and speaks much more like his classmates and friends than he does his Japanese parents.

In your own life, think about the values and habits you want to have, and then ensure you choose your friends, colleagues, mentors and bosses carefully. My friends and mentors have made a huge difference in my life, both professionally and personally. For example, I was able to succeed as an investor in the early years because a super smart mentor was willing to share his knowledge with me, and encouraged me to have faith in my convictions. I'm eternally grateful. Similarly, in my personal life, when I spend time with people I respect, like, and care about, I usually feel great.

To build trusting friendships, I've learned, it's critical to be true to my passions, and express how I feel and what I want. If I weren't open and honest, I wonder what sort of friends I'd have?

This matters. Real friends - people you trust, respect, laugh with, and can rely on - are a vitally important part of life. No matter how much wealth or fame you accumulate, if you don't have true friends it's unlikely you'll be happy. Sadly I know too many people who have achieved their material goals, but have no friends. As the expression goes: greed is a hole you can never fill (though there are definitely a lot of people who try).

Warren Buffett refers to Rose Blumkin, a woman who escaped the Nazis before immigrating to America and founding Nebraska Furniture Mart, as having the ultimate standard for friendship. Ms. Blumkin apparently said she had a hard time making friends. She would ask herself: if the Nazis were to return, would a particular person hide her?

Now that's a super-high standard, but you can imagine how much richer and easier your life would be with even a handful of true friends like that.

View of Husky Stadium, University of Washington.

5

CARE FOR YOURSELF AND OTHERS

Lack of activity destroys the good condition of every human being, while movement and methodical physical exercise save it and preserve it.

- Plato

Our bodies were designed by evolution to thrive on the African savanna. Twenty thousand years ago, people didn't sit in forests or caves staring at computer screens, talking on telephones, or watching television. We were made to move, and our brains were made to think while in motion.

So if you want to feel good, be as productive as possible, live longer, reduce stress, be more creative, and be happier then you need to exercise regularly. When I was at Microsoft, I used to run for about eight minutes every morning before heading to the office. That's not nearly enough, and I slowly got out of shape. I now take an hour at lunch to bike, play tennis, run, or even walk. Over the last ten years, I've lost about twenty pounds and I'm more alert and creative. The extra time invested in exercise has been worth it, even if only measured from a professional standpoint.

Our bodies also weren't designed to eat junk food all day. Thousands of years ago, getting calories was tough; we like sweets and fats now because it was tremendous work getting them then, and we never knew when our next meal would come. While our genetic desires for sweet and fatty foods haven't changed, modern Western civilization, with its easy and rapid access to super markets, processed - and generally inexpensive - food, has removed the natural barriers that stop us from eating what we want. I've always been a fairly healthy eater (although I love desserts!), but one small trick I've adopted is to try to eat dinner early. I've found that just doing that helps keep me at a healthy weight. And, when I eat dinner a bit later, I try to take a walk afterwards.

I recognize that's uncommon. The result of less exercise and more food is not pleasant. As a society, we're getting fat. We're creating many health issues (and costs), which we'll have to deal with down the road.

Another critical element of taking care of yourself is getting a good amount of sleep on a regular basis. I try to organize my schedule to ensure I sleep well since I've learned I perform best when I'm well rested. For instance, when I travel to different time zones I alter my schedule days ahead of time so it's more closely aligned with where I'm going. (I've found that ear plugs are also wonderful tools for hotel rooms if you don't know it will be quiet.) If you can manage to sleep well no matter where you are, you'll find you have more energy and are able to think more clearly.

Stay active. People are like sharks: if we don't move constantly, we'll die. This is true both literally and metaphorically. For example, there's some evidence suggesting that older people who keep their minds active have a much lower chance of getting Alzheimer's disease. People who 'retire' and mostly eat and lie on the couch, aren't likely to live very long -- or be very happy.

Taking care of yourself extends beyond your body to your mental health. Many people don't feel good about themselves psychologically. This may start in childhood when their parents may not give them enough care and attention (so they don't feel lovable); or they may get too much, too easily from their parents (so they end up feeling undeserving). Or their parents may be overly critical; nothing is ever good enough (so they end up constantly trying to please other people, or feeling inadequate, or both).

Regardless, it's important as an adult, no matter what type of parents you had, that you take responsibility for your life. It's only by loving, celebrating, and appreciating what makes you unique that you can fully enjoy your life, and truly love others. If you don't love yourself, the results aren't pleasant. For instance, a number of people I know spend money in unhealthy ways, sometimes running up large amounts of debt by buying things they believe will make them feel better. Sadly, but predictably, it doesn't work. The pleasant feeling of owning something new soon fades, and then they're onto buying the next thing. The debt potentially incurred by this sort of activity not only causes financial difficulties, but may also lead to health issues.

Given the increase in two income families over the last thirty years, you might think that people would be better off. That's not the case. People in the U.S., and much of the Western world, tend to spend more of what they earn than they did a generation ago. They may do this to keep up with their friends, or what they think is expected of them in our society, but that's not a treadmill you want to be on.

People also compensate for not feeling good about themselves by over-eating, drinking too much, over-working, and becoming reliant on constant or unhealthy sex to numb their pain. All of these are addictions. Taking care of yourself means finding a balance that works for you, then having the discipline to maintain that balance. (If you want help, there are many people, including some good therapists, who can be a great resource to discuss issues that are important to you.)

* * * *

Grief can take care of itself, but to get the full value of a joy, you must have somebody to divide it with.

-- Mark Twain

There are innumerable, serious problems in the world, and there are huge numbers of people who'd love your help. You've doubtless heard that message many times before, particularly around the holidays.

But if you need motivation to help others, I can tell you from personal experience: you will directly benefit. Few things make you feel better about yourself. I get great joy out of helping at my kids' school, from helping friends with their business problems, and from doing a good job investing. If I do my job well, my friends and clients will be able to send their kids to college, to retire without financial worries, and to do things that are important to them.

You don't need to look far to help other people. For example, taking the interests of children seriously, encouraging and supporting them, as well as setting high standards, can make a big difference in their lives.

Almost anyone can be a father or a mother, but being a good parent takes hard work, focus, and a great deal of caring. Despite the obvious sacrifices of time and resources, I've found being a parent has been the most satisfying and enriching experience I've ever had. Most parents I know would say similar things.

There are many ways to make a difference in the world – you can help your extended family, help friends, help your community, or help people you don't even know. You can help one on one, or in small groups, or, if you have the ability or resources, on a larger scale. So long as it works for you, it doesn't matter.

When you're in your 80s, and looking back on your life, I have little doubt you'll feel better if you have chosen to give something back. Our time on earth is limited, but you can extend your influence by helping those who will outlive you.

Bois de Boulogne, Paris.

6

LAUGH

With the fearful strain that is on me night and day,
if I did not laugh I should die.

- Abraham Lincoln

While your life will hopefully end better than Lincoln's, it won't always go your way - guaranteed. Within the constraints of your genetic wiring, it's up to you how you deal with that.

You may not have the parents or the siblings you'd have chosen. You may not look the way you'd have picked. The people you love may not always love you back. You may not live where you'd like. You may not have the job you want, or get the promotion you believe you deserve. If you get married, it may not work out the way you thought it would. If you have children, they won't always do what you'd like, and they may disappoint you sometimes.

I've found you can choose to let all the things that go wrong in life depress you. Or, you can accept that things will go wrong, try to laugh, and then look at what you can do. There's a Japanese proverb that gets right to the point: *We're fools whether we dance or not -- so we might as well dance.*

I remember an important business meeting I had about fifteen years ago at Microsoft. It was clear that the problem we faced was unpleasant, and wasn't going away. After a few minutes of intense discussion, the most senior person in the room laughed, and said: "I guess we're screwed!" It shocked me, but that frankness and dry humor immediately stopped the discussion, and we moved on to discussing things we could impact.

A sense of humor is also useful when you make mistakes. I still remember an experience I had during college when I worked as an intern for the MacNeil/Lehrer Report (a PBS television news show). One of my duties was to greet guests at the door. One day I went downstairs to meet Thomas Kean, then Governor of New Jersey. As I got to the guard desk in the lobby, a man walked up and told the guard his name was Tom Kean, and that he was there to go to the MacNeil/Lehrer Report. I introduced myself, and proceeded to take him to the green room to be made up. He kept telling me to stop calling him "Governor" and call him "Tom". He also said he wanted to go upstairs to meet a reporter. I told him we didn't have much time, so he could call the reporter from the green room. When we got there, seated in the makeup chair, he called the reporter and said: "Would you please tell this guy that I'm your boyfriend, Tom Kean, and not the Governor of New Jersey!" I was embarrassed, immediately apologized, and ran back to the lobby to meet Governor Thomas Kean of New Jersey, who stood flanked by two huge state troopers. I remember laughing at myself as I told Governor Kean the story on the elevator back up to the green room.

It's sobering to note that whether you're able to laugh when things go badly may be an inborn trait. A famous study was done using two groups of people: paraplegics and lottery winners. The study looked at these two groups' happiness before their life-changing events, immediately following them, and then also a bit later. The immediate effect was predictable: people who became paraplegics got depressed, and people who won the lottery were elated. But after a relatively short period of time, both groups returned to their original levels of happiness -- paraplegics who'd been happy before their injuries became happy paraplegics; lottery winners who'd been unhappy and bitter before their windfalls became unhappy, bitter lottery winners.

I know several personal stories, including friends who lost a child in a terrible accident (the most horrible thing I can imagine), that illustrate the same principle: some people can laugh even amidst terrible times. The payoff is the physical act of laughing actually improves your mood.

Assuming your basic life needs are being met, you can choose to be happy if you want -- even when you make mistakes, or are in the middle of some pretty awful circumstances. If, however, you're the sort of person who chooses to be unhappy, or filled with anxiety, chances are you'll probably succeed with that as well.

In thinking about this, I keep Mark Twain in mind: *The fear of death follows from the fear of life. A man who lives fully is prepared to die at any time.*

Sunset at the edge of the Glass Mountain Range, West Texas.

7

DO WHAT YOU LOVE

There are but three events in a man's life: birth, life and death. He is not conscious of being born, he dies in pain, and he forgets to live.

- Jean de la Bruyere

How many movies have you seen where the hero or heroine quits a job they hate to pursue their life dreams? These movies wouldn't be made, and they wouldn't resonate with so many people, if they didn't contain an important desire that most people deny themselves.

A lot of apparently 'successful' people believe they should delay enjoying life until later. First they work incredibly hard to get into the 'right' schools; then they work even harder to get a coveted job; and then they work harder still for years to get to a certain position, or make a certain amount of money. The net of this whole adventure is that frequently it's not until late in life, when a person's health may be going, and a lot of their life is behind them, that they stop to think about what they want. And, by then, there may not be much they can do about it. They can't recover the time. And many people don't even stop to think.

Oliver Wendell Holmes noted: *Many people die with their music still in them. Why is this so? Too often it is because they are always getting ready to live. Before they know it, time runs out.*

When I was growing up, someone told me to live as if I was going to die in ten years and had no immediate financial needs. That's great advice. If you can do that, you'll be happier and more successful.

To figure out what you want to do, you need to know yourself. If you lie to yourself about who you are, or hide your identity from others, it will inevitably create stress, and it's unlikely you'll be either productive or happy. Part of knowing yourself means acknowledging what you genuinely want. If you focus on what other people expect of you, you may impress your friends, family and colleagues, but it's unlikely you'll be satisfied with yourself over the long term.

You need to understand your values and your priorities. For example, some people value income more than others, while other people place greater importance on the sense of meaning they find in a job.

Although what makes you passionate generally doesn't change over time, what you want to do sometimes does. When I was young, I didn't know what I wanted to do. I always liked to read, but not necessarily the books that were assigned by my teachers. When I was about 18, I decided I wanted to be a journalist. I always loved learning, and I thought being a journalist would be a great way to stay informed about the world. After working as a journalist in college, I found I liked many aspects of the job, but I didn't think it was the perfect fit for me. I tried other careers through my twenties and thirties, searching for something that felt right. I started a small business (which eventually folded for lack of funding). I went back to business school. Then I worked for two big corporations -- in two very different industries -- Time Inc. and Microsoft. I succeeded at some jobs, and I failed in aspects of others. I enjoyed a few jobs a great deal, and was lucky to make some life-long friends along the way.

It wasn't until I was in my late 30's, when I started to work for myself investing, that I finally found a career which drew on all of my natural curiosity, had few aspects to it that I didn't enjoy, and basically didn't feel like work. Fortunately, everything I'd done earlier in my career wasn't wasted. In fact, many of the experiences I'd had (and particularly my failures) became useful learning.

While it's obviously better to start doing what you love early in life, many people don't. Tom Clancy, the author of numerous exciting and commercially successful books, including <u>The Hunt for Red October</u>, became a writer when he was in his 30's, after a career in the insurance business. John Grisham, the author of many great legal stories, was an attorney and a local politician before his first book, <u>A Time to Kill</u>, was published when he was about 33. Ronald Reagan wasn't elected to public office until he was 55; earlier in life he'd been an actor and a union official. And, though few have heard of Alfred Wallis, merchant and fisherman, art lovers know that Alfred Wallis the painter emerged in his late 60's, after his wife died. So it's quite possible to reinvent your career even late in life.

All of these people successfully evolved their careers toward doing something they loved. But why is that important?

There are three primary reasons:

> We spend huge amounts of our lives working; if you work from the time you're 20 until you're 65, five days a week, (and a great many of us work far more than that) then you will work for at least half your adult life.

> We also live in a super competitive world. It's likely the only way you'll stand out at what you do is if you work very hard for long periods of time. It's said that to become an expert in a given activity requires about 10,000 hours of practice. At 40 hours a week (doing nothing else, which is extremely unlikely) it takes five years of solid work to master a subject.

And I've found the only way people have the stamina to outwork others, year after year, is when they love what they do.

Sadly most people don't have jobs they truly love. Instead, they often work at unsatisfying jobs – sometimes because they have no choice, but sometimes to impress others. But three-window offices, fancy titles, awards, and more *stuff* don't bring happiness. Some people never get this.

I was recently chatting with a guy I met who'd been quite successful. I said I'd been in New York on 9/11, and had heard through a friend he was supposed to have been at the top of the World Trade Center that day, but that he'd fortunately cancelled last minute.

He corrected me: "Actually, I was supposed to be *the keynote speaker* at an important event at the World Trade Center on 9/11."

I was stunned: He'd almost died in a spectacular catastrophe that impacted millions of people, and yet, years later, in telling the story he tried to impress me with the status of his job! I told him I thought he was just lucky to be alive.

There's a lesson here. For people who have a choice between jobs, there are frequently two broad options.

Option 1 is doing what you love every day, but not earning as much money as you might otherwise, and/or not having as much prestige in the eyes of your acquaintances.

Option 2 is doing a job you hate or find boring, but either the job itself, or the money you can make from the job, impresses other folks.

To me, the choice is clear. What I find a bit shocking is that many people choose option 2, and stick with it over the course of their careers. Many other people enter fields they love, but over time forget what they love about their work, and prioritize the external recognition they receive from it. While there's nothing wrong with being well-paid, and we all love to receive praise for good work, prioritizing external rewards over the work itself is a failing strategy.

It's just anecdotal data, but everyone I know who works primarily to impress other people is unhappy or unfulfilled, regardless of how externally 'successful' they may seem. Almost everyone I know well who works passionately at a job for its own sake is happy, and most have been successful.

So the question is: How do you determine what you passionately want to do? I'll share my own experience. Before I left Microsoft, I took out a piece of paper, and listed those moments in my life I loved most. I tried to identify patterns. With that information, and a bit of research about various career options, I picked something which I thought would allow me to do what made me most happy. I also paid close attention, using the same method, to things I didn't like to do, and worked hard to eliminate those things from my life.

You can use this system at any point in your career, but you may have to serve as an apprentice for several years early on doing less than fun things in order to learn the ropes. That's just part of the journey – assuming you work with people you respect.

I developed a litmus test for job satisfaction that might resonate with you. When I was in a job I hated, I noticed on Sunday nights, or returning from vacations, I actually felt sick. Today, because my work and personal life are highly integrated, I work over the weekends -- but I feel just as excited Sunday night as I do on Friday afternoon.

Ideally, you want a job you'd do even if you weren't paid to do it. That's not an economic reality for most of us, but it's the right goal to shoot for. If you can get paid to do what you perceive as play, you have a great job.

Finally, focus on your present situation and your future goals. People like to strive to achieve something new. If you are a mountain climber, as a good friend of mine is, you always look for the next peak.

Those who live in the past tend to be unhappy. No matter how significant your past accomplishments may be, they won't keep you satisfied. A former classmate's greatest days were at school nearly 30 years ago. He went to a wonderful and prestigious school, and was a bit of a star there. These days, he tries to attend as many reunions as he can. But you can't live life backwards, and he's unfulfilled in his current life.

Freud said: *"Love and work are the cornerstones of our humanness"*. While it may sound simple, if you have close friendships and love your work, the odds are quite high that you'll be happy most of the time.

Paris, France.

8

EMBRACE CHANGE

It is not necessary to change. Survival is not mandatory.

-W. Edwards Deming

Change will happen whether you like it or not. In fact, given technology's evolution and globalization, there's little doubt that the rate of change is accelerating. This can be disconcerting; we tend to hate change. We prefer to know what will happen.

However, if you fight change you'll usually lose -- and you'll get worn down fighting it.

I recall meeting with some folks in the newspaper and yellow pages industries in the mid-90's. I told them the Internet would reshape their world, but they were making good money on their print business, and had been doing that for many years. In fact most of them had monopolies where they could pretty much charge whatever they wanted. So, overall, they basically ignored the Internet (they did little things here and there, but nothing fundamental). It didn't impact their near term earnings.

Five years later, nothing had happened to those businesses. After ten years, the Internet started encroaching on their profits. And then, very quickly, the Internet tidal wave decimated them. To be clear: a small number of these companies may still adapt and survive, but had they viewed what was happening in the world with open eyes and started making meaningful changes to their businesses in the mid 90's, I'd bet a lot of money some of them would be in a dramatically different place today.

This pattern of ignoring change is not new. Alexander Graham Bell said: *"When one door closes, another door opens; but we so often look so long and so regretfully upon the closed door, that we do not see the ones which open for us."*

The same is true in personal relationships. If you fight change, it simply won't work. People fall out of love, they age, their needs and desires change. If you embrace inevitable change, you'll be ahead of the pack. If a relationship isn't working, don't just give up. But if you have tried hard to fix it over time and can't do anything about it, then it's important to recognize you may need to make a change in your life.

The lesson I've learned is this: Since change is inevitable, the key is learning how to manage it. If you deal with issues immediately and don't let them fester, they won't become bigger and, ultimately, unmanageable. Problems are much easier to deal with when they're still small than if you you've let them grow over time.

At some points in your life, you may try to drive change. In those instances, I've found patience is a huge virtue. Change comes slowly. It's a hard thing to accept, and people may resist it actively or passively. In fact, in some fields (such as Internet adoption), change often doesn't come until people leave their jobs and are replaced by a new generation. This principle holds true well beyond the technology sector.

Upper West Side of Manhattan
and the Jacqueline Kennedy Onassis Reservoir.

9

LEARN FROM EXPERIENCE

The definition of insanity is doing the same thing over and over again and expecting different results.

- Albert Einstein

While I've met many people who focus on being smart and working hard, I know few people who regularly focus on learning from their own experience and the experience of others. I've noticed that if you are one of those few who try to learn every day, it makes a huge difference over long periods of time.

Many people act like the guy in the story who went to the movies with his friend.

> The guy says to his friend: "I bet the cowboy falls off his horse at the end of the movie and dies."
>
> His friend takes the bet.
>
> The cowboy indeed falls off his horse and dies.
>
> The guy says to his friend: "I don't understand why you bet me. We saw the movie last week!"
>
> The friend says: "Well, I didn't think he'd be dumb enough to do it again."

It's a funny story -- and it seems ridiculous. And yet, I've seen many people over the years do essentially the same thing. They ignore clear lessons from their experience or the experience of others.

If you want to learn from experience, I've found the following useful:

Be curious. Kids naturally are curious and they are able to learn and progress at very rapid rates. I've tried to maintain my natural curiosity as I've gotten older and I've found my life is more interesting as a result.

Read widely. There's so much wisdom written down and it's easier (not to mention less painful) to learn from others' mistakes. No one domain or field has a lock on wisdom. I've been astonished how much you can learn if you read widely across a variety of fields. I read as much as I can.

Find mentors. If you can identify people who have more experience than you and who excel at what they do, it's incredible to have the opportunity to learn from them. People love to teach others. If you're highly motivated, and don't ask for anything other than wisdom you can learn a great deal. Mentors have made a big difference in my life.

Observe. A good friend of mine says people have two eyes, two ears, and only one mouth for a reason. There's certainly a lot to be gained from watching and listening. When I travel, I love listening to people who have different life experiences than I have. I learn so much from them.

Data and patterns matter a great deal. There's much to be learned from analyzing the world. In investing, and in life more broadly, I've found it's important to understand things in terms of systems with various inputs and layers of potential effects. I loved statistics in school and I've found that it (along with psychology) may be the most under-taught academic subject, with the greatest potential gain to society from more people understanding it.

That being said, not everything that's important can be counted, and not everything that can be counted counts. As Mark Twain is alleged to have said: *History does not repeat itself, but it does rhyme.* In other words, just because something happened once doesn't necessarily mean it will happen again in the same way. Otherwise, historians would be among the wealthiest people on earth.

So to understand the world, you need to pay attention to more than simply memorizing a series of events, or existing patterns. Judgment and wisdom matter a great deal. And both require experience and, really, failure. Unfortunately, few of us learn much from our successes.

Even if you make wise decisions throughout your life, you'll inevitably make mistakes. In part, this is because life is not like a math problem with one perfect solution. A lot of decisions are inherently probabilistic and the best you can do much of the time is make a decision that's likely to turn out in your favor. In fact, the harder and more innovative things you try to accomplish, the more likely you are to fail. That's just the reality.

So when decisions, ideas or new projects don't work out, try to learn, and be open-minded. Also, see whether you can sort out whether the idea was flawed, or whether it was solid but the outcome suffered from bad luck.

It's tempting to ascribe things to poor luck that were the result of your dumb decisions. The opposite is also true: sometimes you can get wonderful outcomes from terrible decisions. Although it's incredibly hard to do, it's also useful to see if you can identify mistakes you've made even when things work out as well as, or better than, you expect.

To learn from your experience and the experience of others it's important to try to be dispassionate in looking at the world and analyzing it. You need to be willing to try things you think make sense, and then to admit your mistakes, to throw away your beloved theories, and to learn from other people. This process requires a degree of humility that's frequently lacking in the world, particularly among people who have been successful.

As the 19th century humorist Josh Billings noted: *It ain't what we don't know that gives us trouble, it's what we know that just ain't so.*

Lake Washington, looking back toward Seattle.

10

HAVE DREAMS AND WORK TOWARD THEM

I'm a great believer in luck, and I find the harder I work, the more I have of it.

- Thomas Jefferson

Success in my experience requires the following elements:

- A clear, stretch goal. If the goal is too easy, it won't feel like an achievement; if it's unrealistic, you'll never do the work.

- Love for what you're doing.

- Very hard work, often over a long period of time.

- A sense of realism about the world, and your own limitations. As we used to say at Microsoft: you can't boil the ocean. Nor can you make people come back from the dead.

- Flexibility and perseverance -- you'll need to adapt to the curve balls life will throw at you.

…And, often, a bit of luck.

People don't tend to achieve things in great leaps forward. Rather, we progress one step at a time, usually with small insights here or there. Whether you're a scientist who builds on the great work of others, or a writer whose work springs from the wisdom of writers before you, or an Internet entrepreneur whose innovations succeed only because of a certain infrastructure… all of this is possible only because of small progressions from a massive foundation of wisdom and experience stretching into the distant past. We're all standing, as Isaac Newton noted, on the shoulders of giants.

Similarly, to make changes in your life, focus on taking small steps in the right direction. Whether you want to change your health, your job, or your relationship, you can't do it overnight. And you can't become *great* at anything without a lot of repeated practice.

Be sure you're comfortable with taking small steps, then build on them. The initial change will be small, and in the near term the difference may be imperceptible, but as time goes on you'll end up in a totally different place than where you started.

Having run a marathon many years ago (slowly!), I think long distance running is an excellent way to think about big, challenging goals. If you're out of shape and try to run a marathon immediately, you'll not only fail, but you'll probably seriously injure yourself. If, however, you take small steps, if you slowly start walking, then running short distances, then building to greater distances... over time, it's likely you'll find you can run a marathon.

The same method works for just about anything in life. Faced with a big challenge, you might get overwhelmed, or panic. You might even be afraid of succeeding. As a result, you might not even try. But you can overcome these mental traps by taking small-steps and practicing regularly.

It also helps to *imagine* your success. The mind is an amazing thing. If you focus your brain on success and you practice seriously, you'll slowly build the deep confidence you need to persevere in life. You'll be ready for the obstacles the world throws at you -- or at least you'll expect to encounter them. And, rather than panicking or freezing next time you face a challenge, you'll continue to work toward your goals. Over many years, this type of approach tends to build lasting progress and, ultimately, success.

You need to set the bar high enough that achieving your goals will mean something to you in the long term. And you should ensure that your goals are at least broadly realistic. But you also should try to get on a train going in the right direction.

The Internet provides some great examples of the benefits of having the wind at your back:

If you want to be a journalist, you're likely to be far more successful over the next twenty years if you focus on new media versus trying to become a print specialist. You're also likely to do better designing graphics for the web than you would for magazines, and you're likely to be more successful selling ads for Internet properties and mobile applications than you would for newspapers and TV.

The skills and interests required to succeed in these endeavors are similar, but, if the field you enter is growing, your odds of success will be higher.

I know people who have chosen both paths. Even the most talented and hard-working folks I've observed are constrained by shrinking fields. So while you should pick something you love first, why not try to do that in an environment that will help you succeed?

Simple things can cause complicated outcomes, both good and bad. Persistent curiosity, combined with sustained focus on reasonable goals, will change your life over time. If you love what you do and work very hard, persevere, and take small steps, you likely will be in a dramatically different place ten years from now.

The same is true in your personal life. Picking the right partner - someone you respect, and with whom you can communicate, laugh and collaborate well - can make a huge difference in the quality of your life. However, like a career, long term relationship success requires perseverance and flexibility. People live happily ever after only in the movies.

No matter what your individual goals, hopes and dreams are, I hope you start immediately on your journey and keep going.

Life is short!

As Benjamin Franklin wrote: *"You may delay, but time will not"*.

Whidbey Island, WA.

11

EPILOGUE:
if this book were even shorter, here's what it might say

Everything should be made as simple as possible, but not simpler.

- Albert Einstein

There are certain themes that run throughout the book. It may be useful for some readers to discuss them here.

Know yourself. To be happy, you need to pay attention to who you are, what you want, and how you feel, versus staying busy just doing 'stuff,' or doing what other people want or expect you to do. This requires both self awareness and introspection: if you pay attention to how you feel, what you like and what you want (as well as what makes you feel sad, angry, fearful and confused), the world is likely to look quite different. Many people are afraid of being introspective because they feel vulnerable. But without a willingness to open up, you won't understand yourself and you can't ultimately be truly happy.

Act on that knowledge. Simply understanding how you feel and what you want is vital, but insufficient. Progress depends on action. If your goal is to help other people, but you never do anything about it, you'll be unsatisfied. The same is true if you want to start a business, write a book, invent some new device, learn to play an instrument, get better at a sport, or be a good parent. Remember: take small steps. They work. Big steps often don't. Over time, small steps add up, and you end up in a different place.

Observe. It's incredibly hard to have a dispassionate view of the world, even if you try your hardest. Humans are emotional animals, and we all come at the world with our own point of view based on our experience. It's impossible in many ways to get outside that frame of reference, although with diverse experience, a lot of reading, honest self-reflection on your failures, and some thinking, it's possible to stretch our perspective. Data and patterns matter, and you should pay close attention to them. But they're not enough to deeply understand the world, since history doesn't repeat itself exactly. Judgment and wisdom matter a great deal. To acquire them, and to be creative, it's important to slow down enough at times to notice what is going on around you.

Focus. Focus is important because time is limited and you can't do everything, let alone do everything well.

Persevere. Life doesn't come easily most of the time to most of us. Even if you have no major issues in your life, eventually you will. The way to succeed amidst obstacles is to not give up. Perseverance matters. I don't know anyone who has succeeded over time in any field or significant endeavor without it.

Manage change. Change happens whether you like it or not, both in our personal lives and in our world more broadly. With technology and globalization, the rate of change in society is accelerating. Being able to accept and manage change is an essential skill.

Make friends. Without true friends, most of us wouldn't enjoy our lives. To be happy, it's vitally important to be connected to other human beings whom you care about and who, in turn, care about you.

Care. If you don't take good care of yourself physically and psychologically, you won't be able to enjoy your life. And if you don't care about others, you at least will be missing one of the great joys of being alive.

Judgment matters. This is not a recipe book. Many of these ideas conflict with others. For example, you can't both create space to let your mind wander and intensely focus at the same time. You need to use your judgment to figure out what's right for you at a given time in your life.

Laugh. We're all going to be dead anyway some day. So while you should try your hardest to make the most of your life, when something funny happens, when you make a mistake, or even (and perhaps especially) when bad things happen, it's easier if you can laugh about yourself and the world.

Hiking near Geneva, Switzerland.

12

AFTERWORD
THE WORLD BEYOND US

Money is better than poverty, if only for financial reasons.

- Woody Allen

This is a book about how to get the most out of life. But I don't want you to think I'm some sort of wild eyed optimist who only sees the positive in the world.

We all have problems. People get sick. We die. We get rejected from schools and we lose jobs. We fail at things we try to do. People disappoint us. Relationships and marriages fall apart. Some of us have financial troubles which can spread into other areas of our lives. And, on extremely rare occasions (which are far less likely to happen to you than you'd think reading the news), we're impacted by random acts of violence and terrorism. None of these things are fun; many are painful; and some can be debilitating.

Still, if you're reading this, it's likely you are lucky.

There aren't many statistics in this book, but it might be useful to put the world into a bit of context.

At least 80 percent of the world's population lives on less than $10 per day (or less than $3,650 per year). I don't know about you, but I could not imagine doing that.

About one in four people in the world lack electricity; and one in six people in the world don't have access to clean drinking water, nor can they read, or write, or sign their names. By way of contrast, I don't even think about getting water out of the tap or taking a shower.

Most of the world is not focused on a second car, or what certain Hollywood actors did in their personal lives. They would be grateful for a good meal.

Life is imperfect everywhere. There are real problems in the developed world, many of which you can read about regularly in the press.

The combination of record high levels of unemployment and government debt is a massive problem for citizens and governments from the U.S., to the E.U. to Japan. If you don't have a job, and you both want and are able to work, life is hard.

Environmental challenges are also growing as more of the world becomes industrialized. The U.S. is not leading in addressing this challenge today, but what happens in places like China and India -- with their nearly 2.5 billion people between them -- may matter a lot more.

Weapons of mass destruction could, in the hands of fanatics, severely impair civilized life on earth. The odds of an event happening are quite low, but the consequences of such an event could be catastrophic.

Education is another field that requires focus, as many people in our societies aren't getting access to the sort of educational opportunities that will allow them to compete in the world today, let alone the world in which our children will live in twenty years.

The income gap between the stars of the global, technology driven economy and average workers is growing in a way which could lead to societal instability over time.

Solving or even adequately addressing these issues is not easy. Solutions in a few areas may be unclear, and in other areas the solutions are apparent but they require pragmatic actions that will cause short term sacrifice.

Moreover, most families have two parents working outside the home in increasingly challenging jobs, with the result that many people have more demands on their time than ever before. And of course many households have single parent families and they, too, have increased pressures.

That being said, we in the developed world live dramatically better than even kings did hundreds of years ago. Technology and innovation are rapidly reshaping life in many ways. Both forces have made the world a more competitive place; in many fields today the competition for your job is not simply coming from down the block or across the country, but from around the world or from automation. Few areas of the global economy will be sheltered from these forces, and in fact it's likely that the pace of change will only accelerate in our lifetimes.

There are risks to new technologies, including a potential loss of privacy and various forms of abuse and fraud. However, the same forces are also making our lives more efficient, more personal and, frequently, easier in many ways than they were even twenty years ago.

Job opportunities now exist in the U.S., in Europe and in places like Asia for people who have never had them; the rate of innovation is rising everywhere, and inventions developed in other places will help us all live better too. In addition, global markets are now larger for both individuals with world class talent and U.S. and Western based corporations.

On a more personal level, it's much easier to buy things efficiently, to learn, to rapidly find answers to questions you may have, to stay informed, entertained, and stay in touch with your friends, no matter where they may live.

There's promise on the horizon of major advances in understanding the human brain and genetics which would significantly improve the quality of life for people everywhere. And it seems likely in our lifetimes that we will develop more efficient, greener energy sources which will help power our civilization for many years.

Importantly, we're free in much of the developed world -- something which has not been true for most of recorded history for most people

While our lives are challenging and our world has many issues, some of which are quite serious, problems aren't new to our times, and there are also many great opportunities. Absent humans blowing each other up or some sort of biological catastrophe, life is likely to be much better for our children than it was for us.

13

ACKNOWLEDGEMENTS

Many of my teachers, bosses, colleagues and friends have taught me so much and encouraged me along the way. I deeply appreciate it.

I'm lucky. I was born in the U.S. to a family that valued education and I was equipped with the genetic material to do well in an information intensive world. I came of age in the time of the Internet. I've been surrounded throughout my life by smart and wise people who frequently have given me meaningful amounts of their time, and from whom I've learned a great deal. I've had multiple second chances, something possible in the U.S., but less so in other parts of the world. Had any of those things not been true, I wouldn't be in a position to have the time to learn, to think and to write.

I've had some great mentors. In particular I would like to thank my friend Bob Goldfarb, for encouraging me to become a full time investor amidst the Internet bust and for his tremendous help and support since then. I would also like to thank my friend Greg Alexander, from whom I've learned a great deal, and who has served as an informal partner for vigorous discussion and debate on a wide variety of topics. James Pan helped me understand the joys of running a small investing partnership and has been a source of inspiration and wisdom as well.

I'm grateful to various friends and colleagues, including April Roseman, Rebecca Rubin, Catherine Roche and Steve Moore, for encouraging me to write a book. It wasn't easy, but it was fun.

My friends Lillie Stewart and Jamie Monberg both had unusually good insights and helpful suggestions. They're smart people, who work unbelievably hard and accomplish amazing things, and still take the time to care about their friends. I appreciate it.

Eric Perret, who is a first rate writer, did a masterful job in helping me edit the book. I'm sure the book is not up to Eric's standards, but that's my fault, not his.

Juli Douglas, who is talented in ways I will never be, did the beautiful cover art. Juli always does unbelievable work.

Paige Prill, who has a great book in her some day, was instrumental in helping me think about marketing possibilities and in giving me good editorial feedback on the book itself.

Dean King, an accomplished professional writer, whose books I've greatly enjoyed over the years, provided an interesting perspective on both writing and publishing.

My brother, John Atkins, who is a wonderful writer, a former editor and an experienced and talented business person offered cogent and direct advice, as he always does.

My former boss and friend, Matt Kursh, applied his incredible energy, creativity and great sense of humor to all of his suggestions.

And I'm indebted to the many friends, colleagues and family who took the time to read drafts, and/or encouraged me, and, in many cases, asked good questions and offered comprehensive, insightful feedback and interesting ideas: Gabi, Steve A., Sandy A., Heidi, Lillie A., Sam A., April, David, Jamie, Mike, Pia, Sean, Tom, Nina, Brent, Alex, Jane, Evan, Harrison, Marilyn, Flo and Jo Ann.

If I've forgotten anyone - and I may have - I want to thank you as well. Any errors that you find are mine.

I also want to make one broader acknowledgement: sadly, many people in the world aren't in the position to be able to act on the advice in this book. You need to have water, food, shelter, and safety before anything I say here matters. I'm sensitive to these issues and I know I'm lucky not to be impacted.

ABOUT THE AUTHOR

Peter Atkins is the managing director of Permian Partners, an investment fund he founded in 2001 amidst the Internet bust. Permian approaches buying stock the same way it would evaluate the purchase of an entire business.

Prior to Permian, Peter was a General Manager at Microsoft, where over the course of six years he helped to start, manage and, later, invest in various early consumer Internet businesses, including Sidewalk.com. Earlier in his career, Peter worked at Time Inc. in New York City.

Peter has a BA degree from Skidmore College, an MBA degree from Cornell University and did graduate work at Harvard University.

Printed in Great Britain
by Amazon

77373650R00036